Introduction

THE Garden of the Royal Horticultural Society at Wisley is a unique blend of the beautiful and the instructive. For over eighty years, it has been a source of inspiration, practical example and advice to members of the Society and it has become a mecca for gardeners and garden-lovers everywhere. The Alpine Meadow, carpeted with wild daffodils in spring, and Battleston Hill, brilliant with rhododendrons in early summer, are just two features for which the Garden is famous. There are many others: the Rock Garden, jewelled with flowers in April and May, contrasts with the cooler attractions of the Wild Garden and its long succession of plants; the Herbaceous Borders and Rose Gardens are ablaze with colour from high summer into autumn, when the Fruit Field and Model Gardens reach their most productive; and the trees and shrubs of Seven Acres put on a fine winter display, while the Glasshouses offer shelter to both plants and people throughout the seasons.

The Royal Horticultural Society came to Wisley in 1904, although at that time only a small part of the 60-acre (24-ha.) estate was actually cultivated as a garden, the remainder consisting largely of wooded farmland. The original garden was the creation of George Ferguson Wilson – businessman, scientist, inventor and keen gardener and, by coincidence, a former Treasurer of the Society. In 1878, he had purchased the site and established the "Oakwood experimental garden", with the idea of making "difficult plants grow successfully". His hopes were so amply fulfilled that the garden soon became renowned for its collections of lilies, gentians, Japanese irises, primulas and water plants, all looking quite at home in an informal woodland setting. The present Wild Garden at Wisley is the direct descendant of Oakwood and, despite great changes since Wilson's day, it is still true to his concept.

Wilson's association with Wisley lasted until his death in 1902. Oakwood and the adjoining Glebe Farm were then bought by Sir Thomas Hanbury, a wealthy Quaker who had founded the celebrated garden of La Mortola, on the Italian Riviera (with which the RHS remains closely concerned). In 1903, Sir Thomas presented the Wisley estate in trust to the Royal Horticultural Society, for its perpetual use. This magnificent gift came "as a complete surprise" and was accepted by the Society's Council with "Applause" – a form of expression seldom recorded in its minutes.

Nothing could have been more providential in the circumstances. For at least thirty years, the Society had been seeking a larger garden "beyond the radius of the London smoke", to replace the garden at Chiswick which it had leased since 1822. It was also committed to building a new exhibition hall and offices and the construction work had already started. Both projects were seen as a fitting way to celebrate the Society's forthcoming centenary, in 1904, but there had been heated arguments among the Fellows (as members were known) over which should have priority and the costs involved. Sir Thomas's generous donation solved these problems at a stroke. By May 1904, the move from Chiswick to Wisley was complete and, in July, the new headquarters at Vincent Square, Westminster, were officially opened by King Edward VII – both accomplished just in time to mark the centenary as promised.

Over 6,000 people visited Wisley during its first year under the Society's control (the figure has increased a hundredfold today) and those who criticized its inaccessible position were quickly silenced by "the great development of road traction". There were others, however, who considered the soil and situation of Wisley most unsuitable for a garden. The soil is mainly acid sand, which is poor in nutrients and fast draining, although in places well supplied with water. Lying in the valley of

OPPOSITE: looking from the Wild Garden to the Alpine Meadow, with the brilliantly coloured azalea, *Rhododendron* 'Amoenum', in front

the River Wey, the Garden is vulnerable to frequent harsh frosts, often continuing into May and early June, and it is also exposed to biting northeast winds. Wisley has been hit by freak weather on several occasions. In July 1965, a tornado devastated the Fruit Field; and more recently, in October 1987 and January 1990, the great storms which swept across Britain resulted in the loss of hundreds of trees, leaving a trail of destruction on Battleston Hill and in the Wild Garden and Pinetum. Growing conditions at Wisley are certainly not easy, but in this respect it is an ideal testing ground for plants: if they succeed here, they will (except for lime-hating plants) have a good chance of succeeding almost anywhere in Britain.

The Long Ponds at the foot of the Rock Garden (see p. 51)

The Society acquired Wisley at a time when rock gardening was very much in fashion and the construction of the Rock Garden was its first major undertaking, in 1911. Other areas of the Garden were already being developed: the somewhat overgrown Wild Garden was cleared, a range of glasshouses was erected, Seven Acres, the Pinetum and Howard's Field were planted and the rose borders were established on Weather Hill. Wisley was taking shape as an ornamental garden, but its educational role was never forgotten, for the terms of the Hanbury Trust made clear that the Society was permitted "to use and occupy the Wisley Estate . . . for the purpose of an Experimental Garden and the Encouragement and Improvement of Scientific and Practical

Horticulture in all its branches". To this end, a small laboratory was opened, later to be incorporated in the romantic, half-timbered, Tudor-style building of 1916; the School of Horticulture was founded; and the trials of flowers, vegetables and fruit, which have been such an important part of the Society's work since 1860, were resumed and expanded.

Today, the Laboratory houses the administrative staff and advisory officers of the Society. The latter provide a valuable service for members, answering thousands of queries on plant identification, pests and diseases, soil improvement and general gardening problems. Both scientific and garden staff give talks, hold demonstrations of techniques such as planting, pruning and propagation and conduct garden walks. Scientific investigation and horticultural research are also carried out, though on a more limited scale than in the past. One of the most significant breakthroughs in this sphere came in 1917 from a former student at Wisley, James Ramsbottom, who perfected a method of controlling the narcissus eelworm and thus revolutionized the daffodil industry.

In addition to all their other duties, the staff are involved in running the School of Horticulture and organizing examinations. The School was set up in 1907 to instruct young people in the principles of horticulture and prepare them for the career of professional gardener. It was a continuation of the Society's traditional responsibility for horticultural education, stretching back to the 1820s when "labourers" (as they were then called) were first invited to train at the Chiswick garden. Among those early student gardeners were Joseph Paxton, who was later knighted for designing the Crystal Palace, and the great plant-hunter, Robert Fortune. At Wisley, too, many leading horticulturists have benefited from the School of Horticulture. However, owing to the dwindling number of applicants, the two-year course has now been replaced by a one-year course, as an integrated part of other schemes of horticultural education.

The main trials ground at

Wisley is the Portsmouth Field, which occupies about 4 acres (1·5 ha.) and accommodates all the trials, apart from those of woodland plants on Battleston Hill and of tender plants under glass. The trials of ornamental plants and vegetables "epitomize . . . the Society's endeavour to show to the public the best kinds of plants to grow" and have always been one of the principal objects of the Garden. For visitors, of course, the trials also offer the chance to see an unrivalled collection of cultivars of a particular plant and to compare, assess or simply admire them. That special combination of learning with pleasure is the essence of Wisley itself.

It is a far cry from Wilson's Oakwood to the Garden of the present, which occupies approximately 240 acres (97 ha.) and attracts almost three quarters of a million visitors each year. Like any garden, Wisley is a dynamic place: the recent storms, devastating though they were, have acted as a facelift, speeding up the pace of change and giving scope to rethink and redevelop major areas – notably Howard's Field, with the new heather collection, Battleston Hill and the Wild Garden. Whatever happens in the future, we can be sure that Wisley Garden will retain its unique character and charm and remain a centre for gardening excellence.

Looking towards the Laboratory through the wisteria-covered pergola beside the Canal

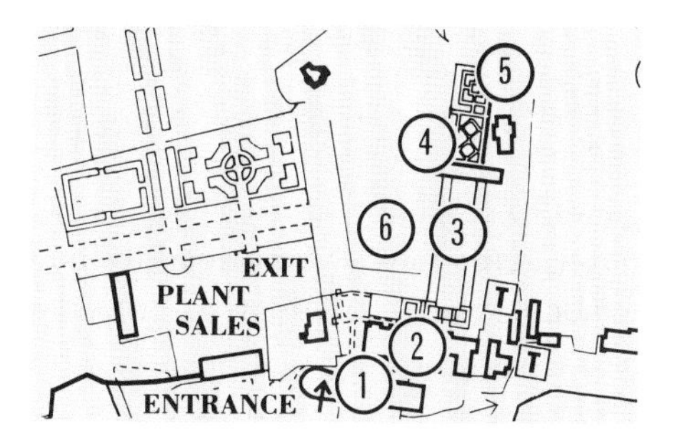

① Entrance and Laboratory ②

PASSING through the entrance to Wisley is like stepping back in time, to a leisured age of large private gardens and spacious lawns. However, the imposing wrought-iron gates, emblazoned with the date of the Society's founding in 1804, leave no doubt that this is the RHS Garden. They commemorate the Reverend William Wilks who, as Secretary to the Society from 1888 to 1920, helped to restore its finances and increase its membership. To him we also owe the well-known Shirley poppies, which he developed by careful selection from the wild field poppy, and these are incorporated in the design of the gates. In the shade of the old oak tree, ground-cover plants and shrubs are happily established – bergenias, *Pachysandra terminalis*, *Mahonia* × *media* 'Charity', *Osmanthus heterophyllus* 'Variegatus', *Euonymus fortunei* 'Emerald Gaiety' and a profusion of ivy.

The sundial inside the gates is a memorial to the first Superintendent of the Garden, Samuel T. Wright, who supervised the move from the previous garden at Chiswick and remained at Wisley until his death in 1922. Seasonal bedding makes an attractive display at the base of the retaining walls beneath the house on the left (where Wright lived for eighteen years). The sandstone walls in turn provide a congenial home for white candytuft, *Iberis sempervirens*, gold dust, *Alyssum* (*Aurinia*) *saxatilis*, aubrieta, *Erinus alpinus* and other crevice-loving plants.

The mellow brick walls of the Laboratory support many climbers and shrubs which benefit from such protection (and perhaps from the watchful eye of the Director in his office) because of their slightly tender nature or early flowering. On the south wall to the right, the large deep pink blooms of *Clematis montana* 'Tetrarose' announce the arrival of summer, before the white, pink-flushed, tubular flowers of *Abelia* × *grandiflora* 'Copper Glow' take over until autumn. An interesting story attaches to the bright yellow *Rosa* 'Helen Knight'. It was raised in 1966 by the then Director of the Garden, Frank Knight, using seed of *R. ecae,* which grew on the wall of his house at Wisley. The new rose, named after his wife, caused quite a sensation and visitors were always asking where they could buy it until, in the early 1980s, it finally crept into the nursery catalogues. The dry sunny bed below the wall is appreciated by grey-leaved shrubs like the handsome *Melianthus major*, with deeply serrated foliage, and is shared by prickly *Acanthus* species, geraniums, the desirable lilac-like *Daphne genkwa*, and *D. odora*, which scents the February air.

Round the corner along the warm west wall, the orange flowers of the hybrid trumpet vine, *Campsis* × *tagliabuana* 'Madame Galen', are a gorgeous sight in August and the yellow saucer-shaped blooms of *Fremontodendron* 'California Glory' (which Wisley helped to bring to the gardening public) are rarely absent throughout the summer. There are several *Ceanothus* species and hybrids, including a splendid *C.* 'Trewithen Blue', as well as clematis, an ancient 'Mermaid' rose, the beautiful *Carpenteria californica*, producing pure white golden-anthered blooms in June and July, and the vigorous *Solanum crispum* 'Glasnevin', with clusters of rich purple potato flowers. A tender spurge, *Euphorbia mellifera*, bears brown honey-scented flower heads in May.

To the left of the front door stand the rare *Desmodium praestans* and the chaste tree, *Vitex agnus-castus* f. *latifolia*, hung with fragrant violet-blue panicles in September and

October. The purple and white flowers of *Hydrangea aspera*, against large woolly leaves, are outstanding in July. Further down, *Parthenocissus henryana* and *Actinidia kolomikta* display their striking foliage and *Azara serrata* contributes yellow powder puffs in early summer. By the archway, *Camellia japonica* 'Princess Charlotte' has been known to open its elegant mixture of pink and white blooms in January, when *Viburnum foetens* makes its presence felt with white, heavily perfumed flowers.

Perennials and small shrubs, many of them the envy of gardeners in colder districts, fill the borders around the Laboratory and supply a wealth of colour in summer and autumn. Salvias, crocosmias and diascias mingle with hebes, rock roses and *Helianthemum* 'Wisley Pink', set off by silvery santolinas, senecios, helichrysums and the related ozothamnus. Two curiosities are *Lobelia tupa*, which has spikes of claw-like, red-brown flowers, and *Cuphea cyanea*, with little red and yellow cigars. In the autumn, the belladonna lily, *Amaryllis belladonna*, unfolds its pink trumpets, along with the more slender *Nerine bowdenii* and *Sternbergia lutea*. Shrubs of doubtful

Abutilon* × *suntense

hardiness flourish here, among them *Prostanthera rotundifolia*, a cloud of blue-purple in April and May, *Jovellana violacea*, with distinctive two-lipped flowers, and the spreading heather-like *Fabiana imbricata* 'Prostrata'. *Abutilon* × *suntense*, hailed as one of the most outstanding hybrids of recent years, provides large violet-purple flowers at the same time. These are followed, from midsummer on, by *Dorycnium hirsutum*, resembling a white-flowered broom, *Indigofera heterantha,* with feathery foliage and pea-flowers, and *Grevillea rosmarinifolia,* carrying a succession of crimson flowers. In autumn, *Colquhounia coccinea* gives a fine display of orange-red, tubular flowers. In the lawn next to the front door, a pool has been filled in and is now used for displays of carpet bedding, which are renewed with a different design each year.

A little detour away from the Laboratory, towards the Conifer Lawn, reveals an interesting group of trees and shrubs – the evergreen maul oak, *Quercus chrysolepis, Osmanthus yunnanensis,* the slender-leaved Himalayan box, *Buxus wallichiana, Deutzia* × *wilsonii,* the graceful *Dipelta yunnanensis* and a tall sea buckthorn, *Hippophae rhamnoides* and, incongruously, a relic of the original Waterloo Bridge.

Ground cover near the Canal: *Rosa* 'Nozomi' and *Juniperus* × *media* 'Pfitzeriana Compacta' (see p. 12)

Canal ③

The Laboratory overlooks a formal canal strewn with water lilies, which is flanked by panels of grass and ends in an open-sided pavilion. This area was the site of the old glasshouses and was re-developed in the early 1970s to designs by the distinguished land-scape architects, Lanning Roper and Sir Geoffrey Jellicoe. Along one side of the Canal is a gravel path and a broad mixed border facing south, composed mainly of summer-flowering shrubs and perennials – buddleias, the hardy *Fuchsia magellanica*, roses, helianthemums, brooms, a double-flowered *Hibiscus syriacus*, the hollyhock-like *Lavatera olbia* 'Rosea', the bright yellow *Piptanthus laburnifolius* and potentillas, with peonies, irises, delphiniums and penstemons. Large specimens of *Parrotia persica* and *Cercidiphyllum japonicum* make an effective back-drop, particularly in autumn with their beautifully tinted foliage. Clematis are allowed to scramble over the spreading junipers and a bush of *Osmanthus decorus* marks each side of the path to the Restaurant. The almond-scented blossom of *Oemleria* (*Osmaronia*) *cerasiformis* is unmistakable here in early spring.

On the other side of the Canal is a pergola festooned with clematis, roses and wisteria. A flowing mass of ground cover, including cotoneaster, junipers and *Ceanothus thyrsiflorus* var. *repens*, conceals the bank, showing how effective this treatment can be for an awkward slope. Near the steps are cut-leaved cultivars of the popular Japanese maple, *Acer palmatum* Dissectum group, and the fine specimen of *Gleditsia triacanthos* 'Sunburst' is an arresting feature with its bright yellow, young foliage.

(4) Formal and (5) Walled Gardens

Beyond the pavilion lie the Formal and Walled Gardens, bisected by a path between clipped yew hedges. Both are on a scale which the ordinary gardener can appreciate. The first is laid out as a formal parterre and used for a variety of spring and summer bedding schemes, creating a rainbow of colour visible from the Laboratory. The south-facing wall on the right houses roses, clematis, escallonia, the rampant *Celastrus orbiculatus*, spangled with scarlet and gold seed capsules throughout the autumn, the twining *Schisandra glaucescens*, with orange-red flowers in May and June, and *Carpenteria californica*. In the bed below grow irises, peonies, crocosmias, the dainty *Gladiolus byzantinus*, *Amaryllis belladonna* and its rare hybrid × *Amarygia* ("Brunsdonna") *parkeri*. The

The Frank Knight gate

north-facing border opposite gives a useful demonstration of what will succeed in such an aspect, with *Ilex × altaclerensis* 'Silver Sentinel' in the corner, *Mahonia × media* 'Charity', a large, variegated Japanese angelica tree, *Aralia elata* 'Variegata', and the rampageous *Lonicera japonica* var. *halliana* clothing the wall.

An archway draped with roses leads to the second, more intimate, Walled Garden. The beds are arranged round a central fountain and planted with old and modern shrub roses, whose soft colours are enhanced by grey and silver foliage plants, blending with phlox, irises, columbines, scabious, lilies, day lilies, agapanthus and Japanese anemones to give a cottage-garden atmosphere. The strange *Lobelia tupa* and the dangling, pale yellow flowers of *Kirengeshoma palmata* strike a more unexpected note in autumn. The Chinese gooseberry, *Actinidia chinensis*, the exuberant evergreen *Holboellia latifolia*, the boldly variegated *Hedera canariensis* 'Variegata' and *H. colchica* 'Sulphur Heart' and the extremely narrow-leaved *H.* 'Bill Archer', roses and clematis clamber over the walls, with *Piptanthus laburnifolius* beneath and an excellent *Robinia pseudoacacia* 'Frisia' near by.

Aralia elata 'Variegata'

At the far end of the Walled Garden, the double gates offer a tantalizing glimpse of the Alpine Meadow and Wild Garden. They commemorate Ken Aslet, a member of the Wisley staff from 1949 to 1975 and for many years Superintendent of the Rock Garden. The gate in the north wall, framing a magnificent view of Seven Acres, is dedicated to Frank Knight, Director of Wisley from 1955 to 1969. Opposite this is a third

The gates to the Wild Garden

gate, presented in memory of W. D. Cartwight, who worked at Wisley for forty-four years.

Just outside this gate on the right used to stand an imposing group of *Magnolia grandiflora*, believed planted in 1915, but drastically reduced by the storms of January 1990. The southerly side of the wall provides support for ceanothus, roses, wisteria, the lovely rose acacia, *Robinia hispida*, *Fremontodendron* 'Pacific Sunset' and *Celastrus orbiculatus*. The fragrant, pale orange flowers of *Trachelospermum asiaticum* in July and August recall miniature gardenias and *Abeliophyllum distichum* responds to a summer baking by blossoming in January. Clematis are represented by the uncommon winter-flowering *C. napaulensis*, *C. rehderiana*, producing soft primrose-yellow blooms in autumn, and a tangle of *C. cirrhosa* var. *balearica*, strung with tiny, cream, spotted bells from September to March. At their feet is a border of irises, *Tulipa* species, colchicums and tender watsonias.

Conifer Lawn ⑥

Remnants of a small pinetum can be found on the slope towards the canal. It is known as "the Graveyard" – all too appropriately now after the storms of October 1987 and January 1990, when a blue spruce, *Picea pungens* f. *glauca*, was snapped off and several other conifers were lost. However, the area still boasts a Chilean incense cedar, *Austrocedrus* (*Libocedrus*) *chilensis*, which is one of the tallest in Britain at over 58 ft (17·5 m), and a rare *Juniperus monosperma*, with feathery foliage. The border along the lawn contains some fine Japanese maples and one or two old roses.

The Main Terrace, with the Conifer Lawn and Laboratory beyond

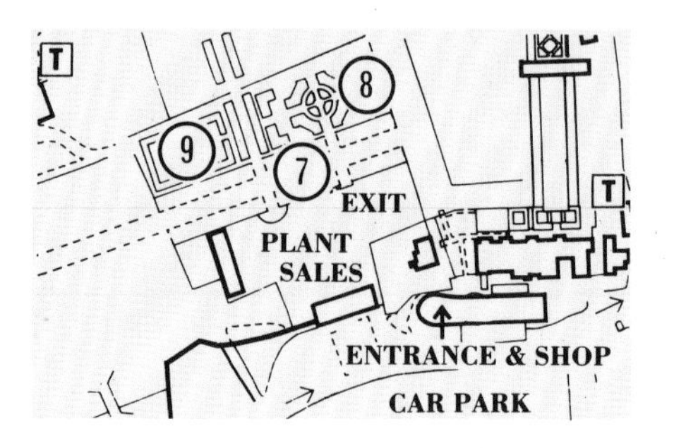

Herbaceous Borders ⑦

THE Main Terrace is a long lawn dotted with circular and oblong beds of spring and summer bedding plants. It leads to the Herbaceous Borders (or, more correctly, mixed borders), which are chief among the glories of Wisley. Each some 420 ft long and 18 ft wide (128 by 5·5 m), they rise gently towards Battleston Hill, backed by hornbeam hedges and with a broad grass walk between them. All the traditional perennials are here – border phlox, geraniums, coreopsis, agapanthus, trollius, red hot pokers, peonies, monkshoods, Japanese anemones, gypsophilas, tradescantias and, of course, chrysanthemums and michaelmas daisies. More unusual are two herbaceous clematis, both with blue flowers, *C. heracleifolia* var. *davidiana* and *C. integrifolia* 'Hendersonii'. The Mount Etna broom, *Genista aetnensis*, supplies some of the shrubby element and a profusion of golden-yellow flowers. For foliage interest, *Acanthus spinosus* and *Paeonia lutea* var. *ludlowii*, both with impressive, deeply cut leaves, are rivalled only by the ornamental grasses, which include the oat-like *Stipa gigantea*, the white-striped *Miscanthus sinensis* 'Variegatus', the blue-grey *Helichtotrichon sempervirens* and *Arundo donax*, the gold-variegated form of the small *Alopecurus pratensis* and the dwarf pampas grass, *Cortaderia selloana* 'Pumila'. Bergenias, heucheras, *Waldsteinia ternata*, violas and other low-growing plants fill every available space and spill over the edges. These are

Looking along the Herbaceous Borders towards the Conifer Lawn

neatly separated from the grass by a line of paving, to make mowing easier; as always at Wisley, there are plenty of tips for the amateur gardener. It is instructive also to see the Herbaceous Borders earlier in the year, with the plants carefully mulched and supported, before they reach their most spectacular in late summer.

The Herbaceous Borders have been undergoing revision and all the beds have now been replanted according to the new plan, which is based on a graded colour scheme. The main emphasis is still on herbaceous perennials, many of them such sought-after cultivars as *Campanula* 'Burghaltii', *Geranium wallichianum* 'Buxton's Variety', the double white *Gypsophila paniculata* 'Bristol Fairy', *Iris* 'Cambridge Blue' (a selection of the hybrid *I.* 'Monspur') and *Dierama pulcherrimum* 'Plover'. There is a generous sprinkling of shrubby plants, too, in the

Autumn-flowering sedum, agapanthus, schizostylis, aster with artemisia in the border

shape of *Cotinus coggygria* 'Royal Purple', the fast-growing *Eucalyptus gunnii* (pruned to preserve the juvenile foliage), *Weigela florida* 'Foliis Purpureis', *Cornus alba* 'Elegantissima', *Hydrangea paniculata* 'Kiushiu', the sweet pepper bush, *Clethra alnifolia, Hypericum kouytchense,* fuchsias, artemisias, helichrysums, lavenders and forsythia.

Running at right angles to the Herbaceous Borders and towards Weather Hill are two smaller borders designed for late summer and autumn colour. Chrysanthemums and asters are to the fore again, among them the distinctive *Aster lateriflorus* 'Horizontalis', a bush of minute leaves and pale lilac flowers. Rudbeckias, Japanese anemones, *Sedum spectabile,* the violet-flowered *Liriope muscari* and *Amaryllis belladonna* all show how effective such a border can be, even in October. The ground is carpeted with *Polygonum affine,* interspersed with colchicums, whose unadorned flowers were so aptly described in the past as naked ladies.

Paeonia suffruticosa 'Rock's Variety' (see p. 20)

Summer Garden ⑧

The Summer Garden, at the foot of Weather Hill, features plants flowering from June onwards and demonstrates various colour combinations which could be used in a small garden. The quarter-circle beds round a central urn contain seasonal bedding plants. Shrub roses and hardy fuchsias in other beds are set off by a medley of aquilegias, salvias, sedums, bellflowers, day lilies, potentillas, agapanthus, irises, red hot pokers and geraniums. *Artemisia* 'Powis Castle' forms a silvery clump in one corner and there is a fine example of the tree peony, *Paeonia suffruticosa* 'Rock's Variety'.

The top of the Summer Garden is bounded by roses trained along post and wire fences. They include the long-flowering, sweet-scented Musk roses, 'Buff Beauty' and 'Cornelia', with apricot-yellow and coppery pink blooms, the ever-popular, thornless Bourbon rose, 'Zéphirine Drouhin', in cerise-pink, and some of the vigorous, prickly Penzance briers, with apple-scented foliage, which date from the end of the nineteenth century but are now seldom grown.

Garden for New Rose Introductions

The Garden for New Rose Introductions lies to the right of the main Herbaceous Borders and above the Summer Garden. Over 200 cultivars of bush and pillar rose introduced during the previous five years are on view and the garden is topped up annually with introductions from the current year. Once past the five-year limit, the roses are either planted elsewhere at Wisley or discarded. Each year a section of the soil is sterilized to prevent it becoming "rose sick" before the latest additions are planted.

Recently introduced cultivars of miniature roses are grown in a raised bed at the top, while those of ground-cover and new English roses are to be found on Weather Hill (see p. 38).

(A leaflet listing the roses in this section and giving addresses of suppliers is available from the Information Centre.)

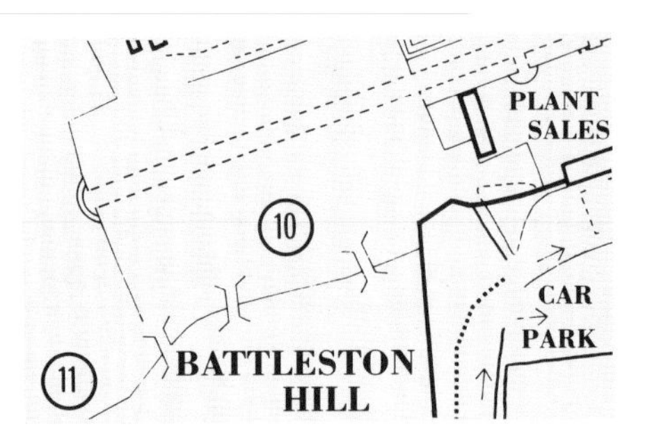

Battleston Hill ⑩

THE path between the long Herbaceous Borders leads to the foot of Battleston Hill, a high wooded ridge running from east to west and falling away on the far side to the Portsmouth Field and the main A3 road. A visit to this part of Wisley in May and June, when it is aglow with the vivid colours of azaleas and rhododendrons, is an unforgettable experience.

Hardy hybrid rhododendrons (what might be thought of as the "typical" rhododendron) grow to the left of the broad walk up the hill. They consistute a permanent trial and are a showcase for many excellent cultivars which have received awards from the Society, as well as promising kinds still awaiting the judgement of the Rhododendron and Camellia Committee. Further up are three beds of smaller rhododendron hybrids, in particular the progeny of *R. yakushimanum*, which have been on trial since 1973. Low-growing, compact, hardy and floriferous, they have everything to recommend them for the smaller garden. On Battleston Hill, they should perform even better after the loss of two large overhanging oaks in the 1987 storm.

To the right of the main walk is the trial of evergreen hybrid azaleas, largely derived from *R. kaempferi*. Prominent among them are the Kurume azaleas, introduced in 1918 from a Japanese nursery by the famous plant collector, E. H. Wilson, and considered by him "the loveliest of all Azaleas". These are at their peak in May, when the little bushes are covered in a profusion of small white, pink, red or purple flowers.

Although rhododendrons are the stars of Battleston Hill, there is much else to ensure variety and prolong the season of interest. Camellias and magnolias open the year: among them are many *Camellia japonica* cultivars, several examples of the bestselling *C.* × *williamsii* 'Donation', producing superb silver-pink blooms in March and April, its sibling, the pendulous lilac-rose 'Caerhays' over the crest of the hill, *Magnolia* × *soulangeana* near by and *M.* × *loebneri* 'Leonard Messel'. The large white snowdrops of *Halesia monticola* var. *vestita,* half-way up on the left, appear in May, when the charming *Enkianthus campanulatus* opposite bears clusters of cup-shaped flowers, yellowish white veined with red, and *Fothergilla major* displays its curious white bottle-brushes. Both the latter develop yellow and red foliage in autumn, to add to the riot of colours provided by the leaves of Japanese and Canadian maples, *Cercidiphyllum japonicum,* a small *Liquidambar*

'Star Shadows', one of the many *Camellia japonica* cultivars grown on Battleston Hill

styraciflua 'Lane Roberts' and the deciduous azaleas. Pride of place at that time of year used to go to *Sorbus* 'Joseph Rock'. The original plant, from which all others have been propagated, has sadly succumbed to fireblight, but its progeny are some of the finest trees for small gardens, creating a symphony of autumn tints with their fruits and leaves.

The lilies scattered throughout the woodland are mostly hybrids, too numerous to mention but including the famous rich orange 'Enchantment', the Bellingham hybrids and the group bred by Dr C. North of the Scottish

Tovara virginiana **'Painter's Palette' and *Hydrangea paniculata* 'Floribunda'**

Horticultural Research Institute in the 1970s. In summer, these compose an inviting picture with fuchsias, potentillas, hypericums, hostas, day lilies, red hot pokers, astilbes and agapanthus. Hydrangeas are well represented, not only the familiar mop-heads and lacecaps, but also the lovely forms of *H. paniculata*, particularly by the curving path at the foot of Battleston Hill. In a damp patch on the corner, *Gunnera manicata* unfurls its enormous leaves amid moisture-loving perennials – candelabra primulas, astilbes and the umbrella plant, *Peltiphyllum peltatum* – and, in September, sprays of yellow shuttlecock flowers dangle from *Kirengeshoma palmata*. On the other side of the walk is a multi-coloured mass of the well-named *Tovara virginiana* 'Painter's Palette'.

Higher up on the left, a series of terraces accommodates miniature evergreen azaleas and creeping shrubs which share their liking for a peaty soil, such as *Gaultheria procumbens*, *Arctostaphylos californica* 'Wood's Red' and *A. myrtifolia*, *Vaccinium macrocarpon*, *Andromeda polifolia* 'Macrophylla' and × *Gaulnettya* 'Pixie'.

Battleston Hill bore the full brunt of the storm in October 1987 and the familiar view from the Herbaceous Borders, with Scots pines and oaks outlined against the horizon, has gone for ever. A notable casualty was *Eucalyptus dalrympleana*, which had reached a height of nearly 70 ft (21 m) in less than thirty years and used to shed its pale peeling bark all around. The tall *Magnolia sprengeri* var. *elongata* and the rare bitternut hickory, *Carya*

OPPOSITE: after the great storm of October 1987

cordiformis were also lost. Especially heartbreaking for the Wisley staff was the devastation of the Dell, the eastern section of Battleston Hill, where so much replanting had been done in the last few years. Fortunately, most of the damage was to the canopy of rather spindly pines and sweet chestnuts, although some examples of the handkerchief tree, *Davidia involucrata*, and *Paulownia lilacina* (*P. fargesii*), with mauve foxglove flowers, were destroyed. It is interesting that the large number of magnolias here survived.

Disaster struck again in the storms of January 1990, when some of the remaining 150-year old Scots pines were toppled; altogether, about 80 per cent of the tree cover on Battleston Hill, mainly on Battleston East, has disappeared. Although major reconstruction work is in progress, the far side is open to the public again and has been made more accessible with a new bridge. Streams and pools are planned, to enhance the different levels in the Dell, and a mixture of dwarf ericaceous plants is being introduced, along with plants noted for autumn colour. Shrubs and trees are being added, to filter wind and cast dappled shade, and shelter belts have also been planted.

Meanwhile, the southern side of Battleston Hill, overlooking the Portsmouth Field, has undergone radical replanting in the wake of the storms and the absence of any useful shade. On the lower steep slopes, a terraced garden has been made with railway sleepers. This is being furnished with rock roses, brooms, rosemary, ceanothus, eucalyptus and other sun-loving plants from the Mediterranean region, Australasia and California, which should relish the sharp drainage and warm conditions.

Winter Garden (11)

The winter-flowering *Hamamelis japonica* 'Superba' in Seven Acres **(see p. 62)**

The main path up Battleston Hill descends, on the other side, to the Portsmouth Field; three wide curving steps, framed with weeping cherries, mark the transition between them. To the left is the Winter Garden, a strip of woodland at the eastern end of the Portsmouth Field, which has been carefully planted to be at its best between November and March. Daphnes, viburnums, mahonias, winter sweet, heathers, Chinese witch hazel and *Prunus subhirtella* 'Autumnalis' enliven the bleakest months with their blossom, often deliciously fragrant as a bonus, and are followed by rhododendrons, camellias, forsythias, the shrubby honeysuckle, *Lonicera* × *purpusii* 'Winter Beauty', and pieris, with their lily of the valley flowers and bright red young growths. The gaily coloured berries of *Pernettya mucronata* 'Winter Time' persist through winter, as do the crab apples of *Malus* × *robusta*. The snaky-striped bark of *Acer grosseri* var. *hersii* seems particularly conspicuous then.

Bulbs can be relied on for an early show, whatever the weather. Snowdrops, crocuses, scillas, chionodoxas, *Anemone blanda, Iris reticulata, Narcissus* 'Tête-à-Tête', the yellow dog's tooth violet, *Erythronium tuolumnense*, and pink heloniopsis grow in pleasant confusion, together with the Lenten rose, *Helleborus orientalis*, and purple patches of *Primula vulgaris* subsp. *sibthorpii*. Colchicums produce their welcome flowers as winter approaches.

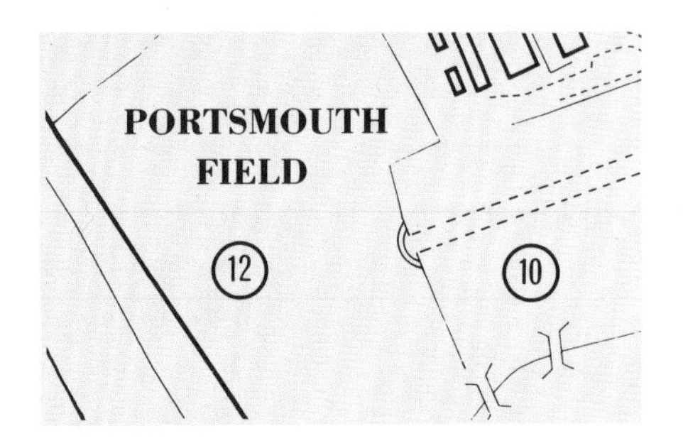

Portsmouth Field (12)

THE Portsmouth Field is the main trials area of Wisley, where plants are grown specifically for the purpose of comparing the different cultivars available and assessing their merits. The trials are of two types – permanent and invited. The permanent trials, which continue from year to year, include delphiniums, dahlias, chrysanthemums, border carnations, garden pinks, day lilies, irises, sweet peas and daffodils. In addition, there are permanent trials of rhododendrons and camellias on Battleston Hill. It is planned to extend the trials to embrace a greater range of woody plants.

The invited trials, which are selected annually, concentrate on annual and biennial flowers, plus a few perennials, and vegetables, and also pot plants in the Glasshouses. It is not always realized that these trials are open to everyone – amateur gardeners, whether members of the RHS or not, and professional seedsmen – who are "invited" to submit seeds or plants of subjects chosen for the year. A calendar of trials appears in the RHS journal, *The Garden,* each autumn.

Entries in the trials are normally sown or planted under numbers, to preserve anonymity, and a detailed record of their growth is kept by the trials department. All plants are inspected by appropriate committees or joint committees of the Society, who can often be observed carrying out their pleasant but very necessary duties, and awards may be given, based on their recommendations.

Descriptions of award-winning plants are published in the Society's *Proceedings* and the trials are regularly reported in *The Garden* and *Newsletter*.

The trials are one of the most important aspects of the work of the Garden. Visitors to Wisley are especially privileged, in that they can see the trials in progress and judge for themselves which cultivar of a particular plant might be suitable for their own gardens. There is nothing quite like the sight of the Portsmouth Field in summer – a sea of blue and white shimmering in the distance which turns out to be rows of delphiniums in flower.

Leaving the Portsmouth Field on the way to the Jubilee Arboretum (see p. 41), it is worth noting a superb specimen of the rare big cone pine, *Pinus coulteri*, which is distinguished by remarkably large cones and spreading bunches of leaves like a chimney-sweep's brush.

The delphinium trials on the Portsmouth Field

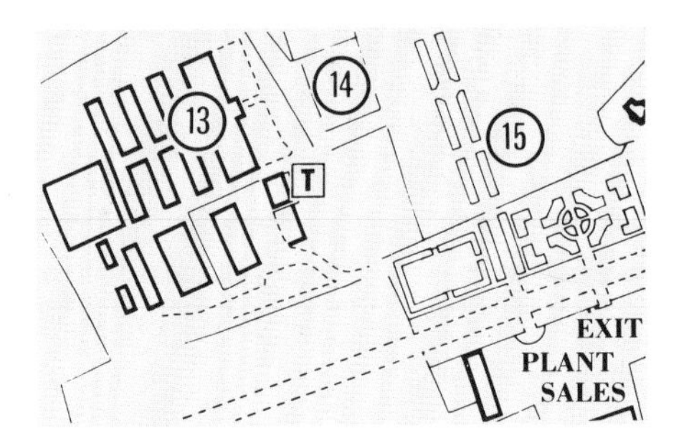

Glasshouses (13)

THE Glasshouses are situated between the Fruit Field, Model Gardens and maintenance buildings and can be reached by a path from the Portsmouth Field or Battleston Hill. The main display house is divided into three temperature sections and the central porch on the north side, flanked by a pair of standard camellias, leads into the intermediate section. This is kept at a minimum of 50°F (10°C), which is suitable for temperate plants, and should provide plenty of inspiration for owners of conservatories. Hibiscus, bougainvilleas, strelitzias, known as bird of paradise flowers, daturas, with great hanging white trumpets, huge stag's horn ferns, fragrant brunfelsias, arum lilies, citrus trees and many other plants from countries a little warmer than Britain luxuriate in these conditions. Passion flowers, including *Passiflora antioquiensis,* strung with dark pink parachutes, are especially prolific and there is a corner devoted to ferns. Houseplants abound, including the familiar cyclamen, begonias, shrimp plants and poinsettias. There is also an informative selection of plants recommended for various temperatures in the home.

The cool section, to the right of the entrance, is maintained at a minimum temperature of 40°F (5°C), which allows a wide range of slightly tender climbers and shrubs to be grown. Among them are the parrot's bill, *Clianthus puniceus,* with claw-shaped scarlet

OPPOSITE: the intermediate section

flowers, several acacias, easily recognized from the clouds of scented yellow blossom, the large South African heath, *Erica canaliculata, Abutilon megapotamicum,* with red and yellow lantern flowers, and bomareas, which resemble climbing alstroemerias. Other permanent occupants are an enormous *Senecio grandifolius,* whose small yellow blooms are borne in large heads like dinner plates, *Euryops pectinatus,* with yellow daisies and grey leaves, *Puya alpestris,* a near-hardy bromeliad which has waxy, electric-blue, unpleasant-smelling flowers, the extraordinary green-flowered *Anigozanthus manglesii,* or kangaroo paw, and *Kennedya macrophylla,* a magnificent climber with brick-red blooms in late winter. A major feature of this section is the seasonal shows of bedding plants and annuals for forcing. In November, the chrysanthemum display, composed of charm, cascade and spray chrysanthemums modelled into standards, fans, pyramids and

The chrysanthemum display

other artistic shapes, is always a great draw.

The warm section, at the other end of the display house, is for plants requiring a minimum temperature of 60°F (16°C) and feels uncomfortably humid to humans. South American allemandas, with flamboyant yellow flowers, and anthuriums, with waxy, palette-shaped flower spathes, passion flowers, stag's horn ferns and other exotica grow in profusion. Bromeliads, that intriguing family of plants to which the pineapple belongs, are represented by garish guzmanias and vriesias and tillandsias perched on a tree. There is a spectacular jade vine, *Strongylodon macrobotrys*, which hails from the Philippines and has luminous blue-green flowers. The presence of such striking foliage plants as ctenanthe, calathea and peperomia may explain why these are rarely happy in the average living-room, unless given sufficient humidity.

Two further glasshouses, accessible from the intermediate section of the display house, are used for trials and seasonal displays, while the small vinery at the far end accommodates a range of grape cultivars suitable for growing under glass. The remaining glasshouses, reserved for teaching, examinations, propagation and growing on, are not open to the public.

However, a stroll through the connecting corridors yields some fine examples of the pink *Bougainvillea* 'Miss Manila', numerous begonias, including a sprawling *B. convolvulacea*, rubber and Swiss cheese plants, ferns and cacti and nerines in autumn. Carnivorous plants are also prominent in the summer. Baskets hanging from the rafters are adorned with the brilliant red flowers of *Columnea crassifolia*.

A path from the back of the main display house runs alongside the complex to a group of smaller glasshouses. One of these holds a large collection of orchids, together with bromeliads and ferns. Cacti and succulents are housed in a smaller wooden structure.

In the borders and raised beds around the glasshouses, amaryllis, watsonias, nerines, crinums and other slightly tender bulbs make a colourful show in summer and autumn, with yuccas and *Abutilon megapotamicum*. Other areas are bedded out with various subtropical plants, giving massed foliage displays. The magnificent new double-span glasshouses (not open to visitors) are a valuable addition to the propagation and research facilities of the Garden.

The Glasshouses close at 4.15 p.m. on weekdays and 4.45 p.m. at weekends and on public holidays.

Model Gardens (14)

Wisley, to many people, means the Model Gardens. Located between the Glasshouses and the rose borders of Weather Hill, they have been created specifically with the needs of the modern gardener in mind and offer a host of ideas and practical suggestions.

The Hedge and Ground Cover Demonstration Area

At the top of the slope, is the Hedge and Ground Cover Demonstration Area. Over a hundred different sorts of hedging plant are on view, from formally clipped to informal and flowering hedges. All were planted in the same year, 1980, so that the rates of growth can be compared. These are interspersed with blocks of low-growing plants, illustrating the potential of ground cover in both sun and shade.

The Model Fruit Gardens opposite are a lesson in how to obtain a good yield of hardy fruits from a small garden. Modern dwarfing rootstocks are used for apples and pears and trees are trained as spindlebushes and in restricted forms as cordons, espaliers, fans and pyramids. Soft fruits – black, white and red currants, gooseberries and raspberries – are grown too, some as standards, but strawberries have been allocated a separate plot, where a system of soil rotation can be practised. Adjoining the gardens is a large collection of soft fruits and some examples of less familiar fruits, such as blueberries and worcesterberries, as well as outdoor grapes, apricots and peaches. The latter are protected with a polythene screen in winter against peach leaf curl. Figs, apples and persimmons look quite content in large clay pots.

The rediscovered popularity of herbs is reflected in the next garden down, immediately opposite the entrance to the Glasshouses. The Herb Garden is formally arranged, with box hedges, urns and a sundial in the centre, and contains a wide assortment of culinary and medicinal herbs, mixed with aromatic plants. Tea and tisane plants, insect-repelling plants and economic plants are given special sections.

Two broad borders flank the path from the Glasshouses to Weather Hill, each backed by a pyracantha hedge and standard trees of *Buddleia alternifolia*, making cascades of scented lilac blossom in summer. The borders are devoted to hardy and half-hardy annuals, both traditional favourites and less common kinds, and present an enchanting display from late June to August.

The Garden for Disabled People has been developed to highlight features and techniques which

Part of the Model Fruit Gardens

may be helpful to less mobile and elderly gardeners. Raised beds for fruit, vegetables and herbs can be tended without stretching or from a wheelchair, while troughs bring alpines to a convenient height. Ramps give easy access to different parts of the garden and all paths and surfaces are covered with non-slip materials. The small greenhouse, with its wide door and raised benches, is a pleasant refuge in dismal weather.

The three Model Small Gardens below this exemplify garden design on a small scale and meet the requirements of at least three of "the Seven Ages of Man". Furthest down the slope is a rectangle measuring 72 by 24 ft (22 by 7 m), typical of a narrow town or suburban garden, which has been planned for a young couple just setting up home. It incorporates simple terracing and aims to give year-round interest with minimum maintenance. The slightly larger garden next door recognizes the demands of an expanding family, with fruit and vegetable plots, a

The Herb Garden

The Model Small Garden for enthusiasts

bed for growing cut flowers for the house and a place for children to play. Finally, the garden at the top is a challenge to enthusiastic gardeners – perhaps a retired couple with plenty of time to spare – and shows how much can be achieved in a limited space. The sloping site has been turned to advantage with a small rock garden and pool, scree and peat beds, a raised bed and alpine sink and an alpine house, all packed with a diversity of interesting plants.

The garden on the other side of the road was used for filming the television series, *Gardeners' Calendar*, and has recently been enlarged, with the addition of a gazebo and trellis work made for the Stoke Garden Festival in 1986. Three small greenhouses have been erected, for perpetual-flowering carnations, conservatory shrubs and succulents. Scented plants occupy another corner and there is a cartwheel of herbs near by.

Weather Hill (15)

Weather Hill takes its name from the meteorological station which once stood at the top, before being moved to the Fruit Field. From the Herbaceous Borders at the foot, the land sweeps up between two long rose borders to the focal point of the Bowes Lyon Pavilion. This was built by the Wisley staff in 1964, amid some controversy over its design, and commemorates Sir David Bowes Lyon, President of the Society from 1953 to 1961 and brother of HM The Queen Mother (herself a patron of the Society). It is framed by two magnificent Dawyck beeches, *Fagus sylvatica* 'Dawyck' ('Fastigiata'), with a grove of silver birch beyond, complemented by a pair of maidenhair trees, *Ginkgo biloba*, at the bottom of the hill.

Large-flowered and cluster-flowered bush roses, better known as hybrid teas and floribundas, are still the most popular roses in English gardens and Weather Hill is the place to see them growing in splendid isolation, in the accustomed manner. The catenary, formed of twin chains of roses suspended from ropes, has been reinstated and, in high summer, this and the rose borders prove an irresistible attraction. At the top, there is also an area devoted to recently introduced ground-cover roses and new English roses.

The open grassy slopes are home to many noteworthy trees and shrubs, interspersed with flowering cherries and ornamental

Cercis siliquastrum

crabs. Near the foot of the hill on the right, *Buddleia alternifolia* forms a beautiful low tree laden with soft purple blossom in June. Close by, *Magnolia liliiflora* 'Nigra' opens large, deep purple flowers in May. The Judas tree, *Cercis siliquastrum,* produces tufts of rosy red flowers direct from the wood before the heart-shaped leaves appear and, in June, *Cornus kousa* var. *chinensis* is wreathed in a mass of white bracts, giving way to brilliant red foliage in October, when the leaves of the red bud maple, *Acer trautvetteri,* turn butter yellow. There is also a splendid, broad-crowned Indian bean tree, *Catalpa bignonioides.*

On the other side of the walk stands a majestic black walnut, *Juglans nigra,* and higher up, the twisted branches of *Robinia pseudoacacia* 'Tortuosa' make an interesting silhouette. In June, the golden pineapple-scented flowers and silvery leaves of *Cytisus battandieri* are particularly striking, as are the bright yellow fronds of *Gleditsia triacanthos* 'Sunburst'.

Catalpa bignonioides

Two shapely specimens of the uncommon *Phellodendron amurense* var. *sachalinense* can be found near by. Above these are the Kentucky coffee tree, *Gymnocladus dioica,* with handsome, large, divided leaves which turn from pink to green, two columnar tulip trees, *Liriodendron tulipifera* 'Fastigiata', and, slightly beyond the Pavilion, the well-named golden rain tree or pride of India, *Koelreuteria paniculata,* bearing deep yellow flowers in summer. In the shrub border grow a number of old roses, underplanted with pulmonarias.

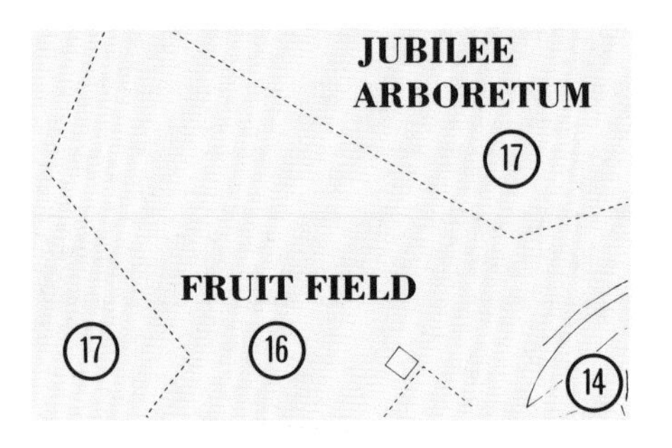

Fruit Field (16)

THE fruit collection is situated in a 16-acre (6·5-ha.) field at the top of Weather Hill, beyond the Model Fruit Gardens and Glasshouses. Half of it is taken up with apples, comprising over 670 cultivars, the majority of which were planted in the early 1950s. They are on 'Malling 7' and 'Malling Merton 106' semi-dwarfing rootstocks (recommended for small early-fruiting trees) and are divided into eating and cooking apples, arranged according to their season of ripening. There is also a block of virus-tested apples on the dwarfing 'Malling 26' rootstock.

Ninety of the leading cultivars of pear are grown on 'Quince A' rootstock, again grouped by season. A similar number of dessert plums and gages are grafted on the semi-dwarfing rootstock 'St Julien A', which is generally considered the most satisfactory, and are trained as pyramids. These have replaced the trees which were badly damaged in the tornado of 1965. Luckily, the Fruit Field suffered relatively lightly in the storm of October 1987, but a shelter belt has been planted to replace the Monterey pines at the western end.

Strawberries, black currants, quinces, various hybrid berries and nuts are grown in the Fruit Field, while blackberries and loganberries occupy two parallel fences just inside the gates. There are also examples of restricted tree forms suitable for walls, such as fans, espaliers and cordons. A small vineyard contains both

Apple-picking time in the Fruit Field

dessert and wine-making cultivars of outdoor grapes.

Because of the Garden's susceptibility to spring frosts, national fruit trials are no longer carried out at Wisley. However, it remains a valuable reference collection, for new cultivars are constantly being added so that their qualities can be compared with those of the older established kinds.

Jubilee Arboretum (17)

The Jubilee Aboretum covers some 32 acres (13 ha.) of undulating land around the Fruit Field and was developed to mark the Silver Jubilee of Queen Elizabeth II. It was opened on 8 May 1978 by Her Majesty and HRH Prince Philip, who planted the first two trees – a pair of upright purple beeches, *Fagus sylvatica* 'Dawyck Purple', each side of the entrance. (Fittingly enough, 1978 was also the centenary of the first plantings at Wisley by G. F. Wilson.) A columnar English oak, *Quercus robur* f. *fastigiata*, was the third tree to be planted, at the end of the broad lime avenue into the Arboretum; it commemorates Bert Pullinger, who worked at Wisley for over half a century. Many of the trees were donated by the famous Hampshire nursery of Hillier, when the firm was forced to reduce its enormous range of trees and shrubs, and the Society owes much to the generosity of the late Sir Harold Hillier. Although the main planting is now complete, a good deal of infilling with trees and complementary shrubs has still to be done. A series of grass-land rides directs visitors to the most important features.

The Arboretum, like Wisley itself, has been planned to combine beauty with education and has three major interwoven themes. The first groups trees according to their season of interest and, in this way, maintains a year-round display throughout the area. Autumn colour, for example, is supplied by the gloriously tinted leaves of *Nyssa sylvatica*, *Liquidambar styraciflua* and *Amelanchier lamarckii* at the far end, where the spectacle can be enjoyed even by motorists on the A3.

The second theme links trees on the basis of their common characteristics, such as shape, colour and type of foliage and flowers. It has already been put into practice with weeping trees, columnar trees, including fastigiate forms of oak, maple and *Ginkgo biloba*, and trees with variegated leaves and will be extended to separate sections for trees with coloured, aromatic and divided foliage and with scented flowers. This system of planting is not only ornamental, but extremely useful to ordinary gardeners faced with the task of choosing a tree for their own gardens. A range of trees sharing a particular attribute can be assessed on the spot and their habits and rates of growth compared, which is certainly easier than studying a bewildering array of descriptions in a nursery catalogue.

The third theme of the Arboretum is botanical, although again helpful to gardeners. In this case, a small genus is selected and all its species and cultivars are planted together. Obviously, this would not be feasible with a large genus like *Quercus*, numbering about 600 species, but with a small genus such as *Catalpa* it is both effective and instructive.

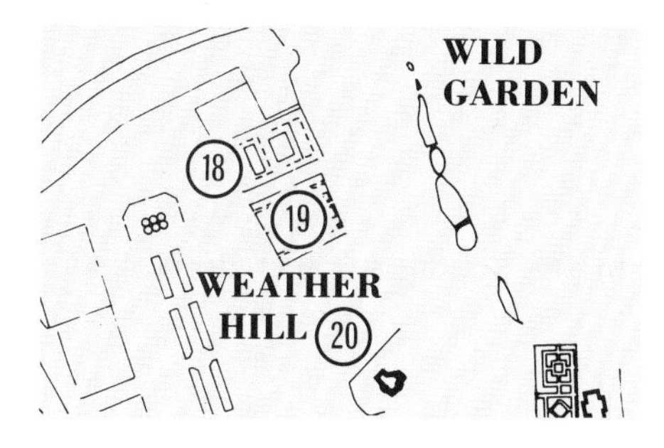

Alpine Houses (18)

THE Alpine House area lies above the Rock Garden, over the crest of Weather Hill and next to the Model Vegetable Garden. Two new houses, completed in 1984, replace the original alpine house of 1926 and the surroundings have been totally redeveloped.

The site faces north and is divided into three levels by dry-stone walls, each constructed of a different local stone – Purbeck stone at the top, Devon slate from Tavistock in the middle, Sussex sandstone at the bottom. The crevices in the walls accommodate a wealth of plants, from lewisias, convolvulus, zauschnerias, hostas and ferns higher up, to the shade-loving *Ramonda myconi*, with lavender-blue, saucer-shaped blooms, and its paler-flowered relative, *Haberlea rhodopensis*, in the lowest and darkest spots.

The traditional wooden alpine house on the top terrace is used for alpines grown in pots. These are plunged into sand on the benches to keep watering to a minimum and, apart from the permanent planting of miniature conifers, are changed according to season. New or reintroduced species collected from mountains all over the world are represented, together with early-flowering plants which can be grown to perfection when sheltered from winter weather. *Crocus sieberi* and the delightful cultivars of *C. chrysanthus* make their début at the beginning of the year, to be joined by tender cyclamen like *C. pseudibericum*, *C. persicum* and the rare *C. trochopterantherum*, *Scilla tubergeniana (S. mischtschenkoana)*, the star-like *Ipheion* 'Wisley Blue' and the diminutive white or pink buttercup, *Ranunculus calandrinioides*. Above the house is a south-facing cliff of tufa, a very porous limestone in which many fascinating plants flourish. A long raised bed near by suits both sun- and shade-lovers and a similar mixture of plants, including ferns, orchids, trilliums, phlox, violas, daphnes and gypsophilas, is distributed in narrow beds above and below the wall.

In the aluminium alpine house on the middle terrace, a landscaped setting has been achieved with soil and rocks, covered with a layer of stone chippings to ensure good drainage in winter, yet retain moisture in summer. Alpine gems from the highest altitudes predominate, notably androsaces, dionysias, drabas and aquilegias, together with silvery-foliaged helichrysums. The choice, but difficult to please *Daphne genkwa*, the scarlet-flowered *Monardella macrantha*, resembling a petite monarda, and *Convolvulus sabatius*, with silky purple-blue

A group of troughs on the lower terrace

The traditional wooden alpine house

flowers, relish these conditions too. All is carefully controlled to meet their exacting requirements and a dehumidifier operates on cold damp days. An interesting range of dwarf shrubs grows in the border below the house – spiraeas, daphnes, box, willows, hebes, spruces, the tiny-leaved holly, *Ilex crenata* 'Helleri', and the pygmy *Cedrus libani* 'Sargentii'.

The hypertufa sinks and stone troughs on the lower terrace are ideal for small slow-growing alpines, such as sempervivums, sedums, saxifrages, silenes, phlox, campanulas and androsaces, which nestle between pieces of rock and slate and maintain a succession of bloom throughout the year. One minute trough is devoted entirely to silver saxifrages. More vigorous plants fill the gaps in the paving, which is a creamy-buff colour to heighten the impression of light, while ferns, hellebores and purple-black-leaved ophiopogons grace the border below the lowest wall.

The Alpine Houses close at 4.15 p.m. on weekdays, 4.45 p.m. at weekends and public holidays.

Model Vegetable Garden (19)

The Model Vegetable Garden is separated from the Alpine Houses just above by a yew hedge and a broad stone path, which opens out beyond an old oak tree to reveal a panorama of the Rock Garden and Wild Garden. The borders each side of the path, known as the Monocot Borders, concentrate on one of the two great classes of flowering plants – the monocotyledons. Day lilies, irises, agapanthus, yuccas, *Phormium tenax*, the silvery-leaved cardoon, ornamental grasses and bamboos all make a rich spectacle in summer and autumn.

The largest plot in the Model Vegetable Garden measures 90 by 30 ft (27 by 9 m) and is intended to show how an average family can be kept supplied with all the essential vegetables throughout the year. A plot of about half this size demonstrates the bed or block system, using 4 ft (1·2 m) wide beds to produce a good yield of salads and vegetables from a closer

The Monocot Borders

spacing of plants than normal; this also avoids one having to tread on the soil, since all work can be done from the paths. Rhubarb, horseradish, globe artichokes and other perennial vegetables have been given their own plot and there is also an asparagus bed.

Protected cropping is provided by cloches, frames and two unheated greenhouses, one of them a "solar" greenhouse made of double-skinned polythene film with reflective shading. Unusual vegetables, like salsify, seakale and garlic, can be seen in the border running the length of the garden.

Bowles's Corner ⑳

A small area in the lower corner of Weather Hill is dedicated to the great gardener, E. A. Bowles, who enjoyed a long association with the Society, from his election to Council in 1908 until his death in 1954, and conveyed his love of gardening to a wide audience through his entertaining trilogy of books, *My Garden in Spring*,

Summer, and *Autumn and Winter*. Bowles had a penchant for what he called "demented plants – departing from normal habit or appearance" and some of these are included in Bowles's Corner. A hawthorn and a hazel, each with extraordinary corkscrew branches, demand a second look, as do familiar plants like *Prunus lusitanica, Symphoricarpus orbiculatus* and London pride, *Saxifraga* × *urbium,* in their variegated versions. In winter, *Garrya elliptica* is draped with long suede-grey catkins and later the donkey's ear snowdrop, *Galanthus nivalis* 'Scharlockii', appears, with long spathes or "ears" projecting above the flowers. Crocuses and colchicums carpet the ground, reflecting another of Bowles's special interests, and many of them, like *Crocus sieberi* 'Bowles' White' and *Colchicum bowlesianum* (correctly *C. bivonae)* are named after him. Several other plants preserve his memory in the same way, for instance, *Malus* 'Bowles' Hybrid' and the stately ornamental rhubarb, *Rheum palmatum* 'Bowles' Red'.

Next to Bowles's Corner is a little arid garden, where euphorbias, grasses and yuccas thrive. The original Oakwood, now called Weather Hill Cottage, lies set back from the path and is a very early example of a prefabricated house. To the left of its gate, a small collection of daphnes has been assembled (one of the genera on which the Director-General of the Society, Christopher Brickell, is an authority). Opposite, at the top of the Main Terrace, stands a superb *Magnolia sprengeri* 'Diva', with deep pink chalices on leafless branches outlined against the spring sky. Round the corner of the house are terraced banks, packed with dwarf rhododendrons and other peat-loving plants – cassiopes, *Pieris japonica,* primulas, gentians, cyclamen, hostas, meconopsis and ferns.

The arid garden

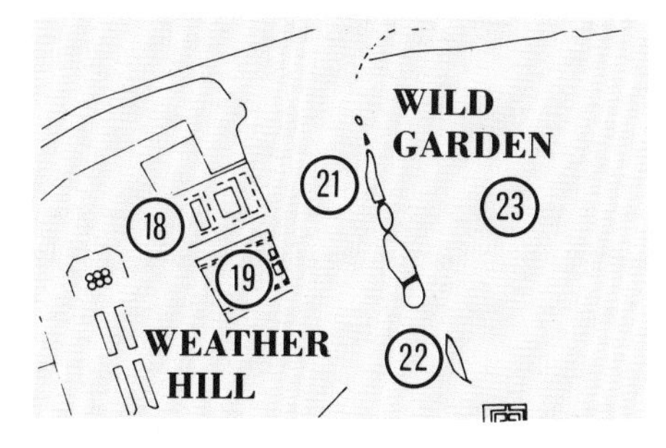

Rock Garden (21)

THE Rock Garden was built by James Pulham & Son, specialists in large-scale rock gardens, to designs by the landscape architect, Edward White, and was completed in 1911 – the first major project at Wisley. During the 1980s, it has been largely reconstructed, using Sussex sandstone from the same quarry near Tunbridge Wells and incorporating new features such as peat beds and a scree. The Rock Garden still slips gently downhill, owing to the light sandy soil and underground springs, and it requires constant renovation. However, the opportunity is being taken to restore certain parts to the original design.

The steep slope faces north and suits many plants which prefer a cool shady spot, as the large and prosperous ramondas in the vertical crevices prove. There is ample room, too, on the more exposed outcrops for sun-loving plants. In April and May, the Rock Garden becomes a treasure trove of gentians, daphnes, drabas, dianthus, pulsatillas, jeffersonias, phlox and countless other alpines, whose exquisite flowers repay close inspection.

Although spring is the main season, it is certainly not the only time to visit the Rock Garden. Snowdrops, crocuses, cyclamen, miniature irises and the scented, creamy-white *Daphne blagayana* begin the year and *Rhododendron* × *praecox*, near the top, lives up to its name with February flowers of rosy purple. Himalayan gentians sport their blue trumpets in autumn and *Polygonum vaccinii-*

folium retains its tiny pink flowers through the frosts, while small evergreen shrubs like *Pernettya mucronata, Skimmia reevesiana* and *Sarcococca hookeriana* var. *digyna* contribute colourful berries and foliage in winter. Numerous dwarf conifers provide a permanent structure, among them the low drooping mound of *Tsuga canadensis* 'Pendula', near the

Pulsatilla vulgaris

main steps, and many small forms of *Chamaecyparis obtusa*, their flattened sprays of foliage giving them a three-dimensional quality. The rare bristlecone pine, *Pinus aristata*, which lent such character to the area, was lost in the storm of October 1987. However, *Rhododendron* 'Temple Belle' presides from a high point, with trusses of gorgeous, soft pink bells in April and roots straddling a large rock in bonsai fashion.

The series of banks at the far end of the Rock Garden offer further variety in the shape of the bristly *Meconopsis horridula*, the most unprimula-like *Primula vialii*, with lavender-blue spikes which emerge disconcertingly from scarlet buds, *Shortia (Schizocodon) soldanelloides* and *Soldanella villosa*, carrying fringed bells in rosy red and purple-blue, the related *Dodocatheon meadia*, with cyclamen-like flowers, the glistening, double white bloodroot, *Sanguinaria canadensis* 'Flore Pleno' ('Multiplex'), and mats of *Linnaea borealis*, the pink twin flower. *Begonia grandis* subsp. *evansiana*, the only hardy begonia, makes a thick clump of green metallic leaves and produces bright pink flowers in August. Near by is an island alpine bed filled with sedums and saxifrages. At the wilder edge of the Rock Garden, snowdrops, hellebores, ground-covering pulmonarias and

creamy-flowered comfrey, *Symphytum grandiflorum,* grow in an attractive tangle.

Several pools at different levels in the Rock Garden are linked by streams and cascades, the water eventually flowing into the Long Ponds at the bottom. These broad ditches between the Rock Garden and the Wild Garden are a haven for ducks and tadpoles and a quantity of moisture-loving plants. No one could miss the huge paddle-shaped leaves of the skunk cabbage, *Lysichiton americanum,* with its bold yellow flower spathes in March and April, or the grandiose umbrella plant, *Peltiphyllum peltatum,* whose lustrous foliage turns red in autumn. Two British natives, the lemon-yellow globe flower, *Trollius europaeus,* and the marsh marigold or king cup, *Caltha palustris,* are happily established on the banks, where *Leucojum aestivum* 'Gravetye Giant', an improved form of the summer snowflake, also flowers

– despite its name – in spring. Primulas of all kinds, astilbes, *Iris sibirica* and sumptuous *I. ensata (I. kaempferi)* cultivars (the latter a feature in the days of G. F. Wilson) continue the display, together with arum lilies, bergenias, hostas, ferns, lady's mantle, *Alchemilla mollis*, and, at the far end a vast *Gunnera manicata*, big enough to shelter under. The rustic bridge over the Long Ponds is draped with *Wisteria floribunda* f. *macrobotrys*, whose beautiful lilac-blue and purple tassels reach down to the water in May, just as they have for almost a century.

Alpine Meadow (22)

The Rock Garden merges gradually into the Alpine Meadow, a grassy slope facing the Wild Garden and dotted with outcrops of rock. On one of these is a spreading, shimmering, blue-leaved spruce, *Picea pungens* f. *glauca*, and two examples of *Acer palmatum* 'Dissectum Atropurpureum' make neat hummocks of delicately cut, deep red leaves, becoming bronze and yellow in autumn. A small collection of bamboos lines the path at the edge.

In early April, the grass is transformed into a sheet of sulphur-yellow from thousands of naturalized hoop-petticoat daffodils, *Narcissus bulbocodium*. The taller *N. triandrus* hybrids succeed them, mingling with blue wood anemones, *A. nemorosa*, pink and white dog's tooth violets, *Erythronium dens-canis*, and drifts of snakeshead fritillary, *Fritillaria meleagris*. In June, the turf is studded with the wild spotted orchid, *Orchis maculata*, and later still, in autumn, colchicums and the purple-veined white goblets of *Crocus nudiflorus* appear.

OPPOSITE: the Alpine Meadow in spring, with the Rock Garden behind

Wild Garden (23)

The Wild Garden is the most historic part of Wisley and, although much altered since the time of G. F. Wilson, it has kept entirely to the spirit of his original woodland garden. In his notebooks, Wilson recorded almost 22,000 separate plantings in "Oakwood", from 1878 until his death in 1902, and it is possible that the flourishing clumps of *Lilium superbum* and *Cardiocrinum giganteum* date from then.

The soil is peaty and more moisture-retentive than elsewhere in the Garden, which was ideal for woodland plants until storms depleted the tree canopy. Other trees now compete in stature with the oaks, particularly the umbrella pine, *Sciadopitys verticillata,* with leaves arranged like umbrella spokes, and *Chamaecyparis pisifera* 'Squarrosa', both of which were planted some eighty years ago, and the fast-growing dawn redwood, *Metasequoia glyptostroboides,* which was raised from the first introduction of seed in 1948, soon after the amazing discovery of this tree. Unfortunately, the sweet gum, *Liquidambar styraciflua,* and a sorrel tree, *Oxydendrum arboreum,* so remarkable for their autumn colour, were destroyed in the 1987 gale, as were a witch hazel planted by Wilson and a strawberry tree, *Arbutus menziesii.*

The taller trees and several more cypresses are grouped at the Seven Acres end of the Wild Garden, where *Eucryphia* × *nymansensis* 'Nymansay', on a mound overlooking the Alpine Meadow, is a fine sight in August, carrying white yellow-anthered flowers among shining evergreen leaves. Two members of a somewhat neglected genus, *Stuartia pseudocamellia* and *S. serrata,* revel in the shade, producing white cup-shaped blooms in summer, and the beautiful snowbell, *Styrax japonica,* is hung with pure white flowers in June. These keep company with the white-bracted *Cornus kousa* var. *chinensis, Fothergilla monticola,* notable for its bottle-brush flowers

***Acer japonicum* 'Aureum' in a corner of the Wild Garden**

and autumn colour, the sweet pepper bush, *Clethra alnifolia*, bearing long fragrant racemes, *Oxydendrum arboreum* and a small paperbark maple, *Acer griseum*.

As in natural woodland, lower-growing trees and shrubs make up the next layer of vegetation. They include numerous *Camellia japonica* cultivars, showing a wide range of colours and flower forms, magnolias of many sorts, starting with *Magnolia* × *soulangeana* and *M. kobus* in April and finishing in late summer with the scented, creamy white blooms of *M. virginiana*, and some massive old *Rhododendron ponticum* hybrids. Close relatives of rhododendrons are the *Enkianthus* species and the splendid *Pieris japonica*, all with drooping urn-shaped flowers in spring, and the kalmias, with pink cup-shaped blooms in summer. The enkianthus develop intense foliage colour in autumn, while the heart-shaped leaves of *Disanthus cercidifolius* turn a stunning claret-red, followed by undistinguished maroon flowers in November.

Primulas at the edge of the Wild Garden

Corylopsis pauciflora and *C. platypetala* var. *levis*, members of the witch hazel family, share their liking for an acid soil and festoon themselves with fragrant primrose-yellow blossom early in the year.

The floor of the woodland is home to an immense variety of plants, which also perform the important service of checking weeds – from shrubby carpeters such as vacciniums and gaultherias, to hostas, pulmonarias, epimediums, tiarellas and the intriguing mouse plant, *Arisarum proboscideum*, whose long-tailed flowers lurk amid spear-shaped leaves. In spring, drifts of *Narcissus cyclamineus* and other daffodils, wood anemones, both *Anemone nemorosa* and *A. apennina*, and hellebores are punctuated with more unusual plants, among them the American dog's tooth violets, *Erythronium americanum* and *E. revolutum*, the wake robin, *Trillium grandiflorum*, in pure white, and the dark maroon *T. sessile* 'Rubrum', *Hepatica transsilvanica*, with large, starry, blue flowers, the crown imperial, *Fritillaria imperialis*, and its less obtrusive kin, the cream and green

F. verticillata and dark chocolate-purple *F. camschatcensis*. The parade of primulas commences before winter is over with the cheerful pink and red flowers of *P. vulgaris* subsp. *sibthorpii*, continues in early summer with the vivid candelabra primulas and closes with the large citron-yellow blooms of *P. florindae*. More difficult Asiatic primulas, like *P. aureata*, *P. gracilipes* and *P. edgeworthii*, are accommodated with a number of ferns in special beds beside a ditch.

In early summer, the lampshade flowers of the blue Himalayan poppy, *Meconopsis betonicifolia*, hover in the woodland, with several less well-known meconopsis. They are joined by the yellow foxglove, *Digitalis lutea*, willow gentian, *Gentiana asclepiadea*, astilbes, *Iris sibirica* cultivars and the prolific white bellflower, *Campanula latifolia* forma *alba*. Lilies grace the scene later on, especially the orange *L. superbum*, the panther lily, *L. pardalinum*, the yellow *L. szovitsianum* and the extravagant giant lily, *Cardiocrinum giganteum*. Campions and foxgloves emphasize the wildness of the garden, as does the lovely white form of the rosebay willow herb, *Epilobium angustifolium*, that common weed of wasteland.

Four National Collections are situated in the Wild Garden, for species and cultivars of *Epimedium*, *Galanthus*, *Hosta* and *Pulmonaria*.

The storms of January 1990 wrought further havoc in the Wild Garden, with the loss of one of its original inhabitants – the famous blue cedar, *Cedrus atlantica* f. *glauca* – and more damage to the tree cover. A large amount of redesigning and restoration is necessary and beds are being cleared and planted in rotation. The long-term objective is to restock the area with hostas, primulas, trilliums and the many other woodlanders that find the high water table and fertile soil so conducive. The replanting on the western boundary in 1988 is already making rapid progress and a bamboo walk is being introduced on the exposed southwest flank to filter the wind. A new network of paths and an irrigation system are also being installed.

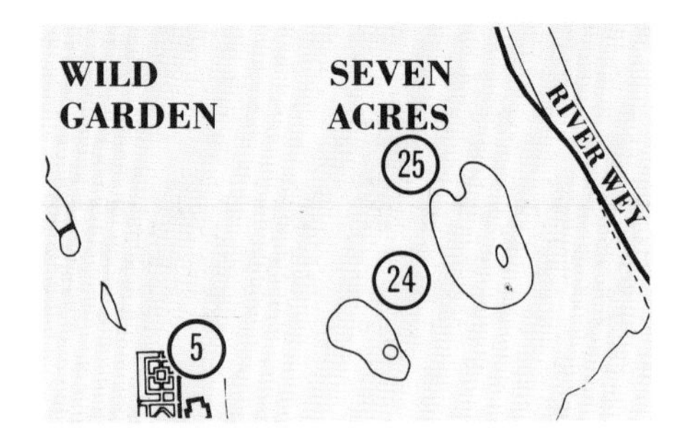

Round Pond (24)

THE Round Pond lies in the middle of the open grassy expanse stretching from the cool glades of the Wild Garden to the Restaurant. Healthy clumps of *Gunnera tinctoria,* a smaller version of the enormous *G. manicata,* and the aptly named royal fern, *Osmunda regalis,* line the water's edge beneath a swamp cypress, *Taxodium distichum.* The superb smoke bush, *Cotinus coggygria,* is enveloped in a cloud of pinkish plumes in summer, followed by flaming leaves, and a fine fastigiate English oak towers above.

Around the base of the silver maple, *Acer saccharinum,* on the opposite bank, the parasitic *Lathraea clandestina* (which grows on the roots of trees) resembles livid purple cushions early in the year. The red and yellow stems of the dogwoods, *Cornus alba* and *C. stolonifera* 'Flaviramea', make a striking impact at the same time and the twisted branches of the hazel, *Corylus avellana* 'Contorta', are noticeable. A strong perfume emanates from the otherwise discreet, winter-flowering honeysuckle, *Lonicera standishii.* The shrub beds near the Round Pond are liberally planted with viburnums and philadelphus, as well as rubus, escallonias, deutzias, weigelas and berberis. *Wisteria venusta,* a climber which is grown here as a specimen shrub and has the largest flowers of all the wisterias, and the charming *Aesculus parviflora,* a bushy plant with white horse-chestnut blossom borne most usefully in July and

Cotinus coggygria and day lilies

August, are of particular interest. *Prunus serrulata* 'Shirotae' steals the show in April, when the spreading branches carry clusters of pendent, snow-white fragrant flowers. In near-by beds, daffodils give way to peonies, bergenias, red hot pokers and michaelmas daisies. Day lilies, *Hemerocallis* hybrids, are well represented, demonstrating their qualities as attractive and reliable perennials.

A group of trees to the south of the Round Pond includes *Quercus cerris* 'Variegata', the rare variegated Turkey oak (there is another in the Jubilee Arboretum), the equally, but more deservedly rare *Cladrastis wilsonii*, which has never yet flowered, and *Magnolia acuminata*, known as the cucumber tree for its short, green, young fruits. The white bark of *Betula* 'Grayswood Ghost' is noticeable, near a bush of *Hydrangea petiolaris*, normally seen as a climber but here grown as a most effective, low, spreading shrub, and a variegated form of the tulip tree.

Towards the edge of the Wild Garden, a large Mount Etna broom, *Genista aetnensis,* makes a vibrant splash of yellow in July. *Ilex × altaclerensis* 'Camelliifolia', which has smooth camellia-like foliage as the name implies, the bright yellow-leaved *Quercus rubra* 'Aurea', *Acer griseum,* with its distinctive peeling bark, and the handsome eastern relative of the elm, *Zelkova serrata,* supply an interesting background.

Seven Acres (25)

Seven Acres is an oblong piece of land of approximately that size (2·5 ha.), bounded by the Wild Garden on one side and the River Wey on the other. Originally rough pasture, it was regarded as useless for cultivation until, in the 1920s, an iron pan was discovered just below the surface and broken up, so that plant roots could reach the moisture. The successful development of the area since then, despite the very sandy soil, is clear for all to see.

The Lake near the centre was converted from a gravel pit. The conical outlines of three dawn redwoods, *Metasequoia glyptostroboides,* are now reflected in its waters, above a fringe of gunneras and small willows. Among the latter, the unusual shining willow, *Salix lucida,* with glossy foliage and a craggy trunk, was a casualty of the January 1990 storms. The whole forms a delightful composition, particularly in summer when the water lilies are out and in autumn when the redwoods are burnished pink and old gold. Around the Lake, flowering quinces, cherries and crabs, magnolias, philadelphus or mock oranges and fuchsias ensure a succession of bloom and, in May, the weeping willow-leaved pear, *Pyrus salicifolia* 'Pendula',

The Lake in autumn

is at its silvery best. Unfortunately, the Chinese fringe tree, *Chionanthus retusus,* which has been likened to a "dome of soft, fleecy snow", produces more of a flurry at Wisley, which perhaps explains why it is seldom seen in British gardens. A little later, the fragrant flowers of the pendent white lime, *Tilia* 'Petiolaris', prove irresistible to bees, which then fall to the ground in a narcotic haze and sometimes never recover. Autumn brings the gorgeous crimson foliage of the sweet gum, *Liquidambar styraciflua,* complemented by the scarlet, orange and yellow of the ground-sweeping tupelo, *Nyssa sylvatica,* both of them relishing the slightly marshy conditions. A small specimen of the uncommon *Picrasma quassioides* also colours well. The tall river birch, *Betula nigra*, and several other trees were destroyed in recent storms.

A collection of dwarf and slow-growing conifers, presented to the Society by A. H. Nisbet, occupies a mound next to the Lake, near the boundary. It contains many rare and remarkable trees, although some have turned out to be not so dwarf or slow-growing and have attained heights of over 20 ft (6 m) after thirty years.

The beauties of an autumn and winter garden are captured to perfection in Seven Acres. The elegant *Sorbus vilmorinii,* in the middle of a heather bed, carries drooping bunches of fruit against fern-like bronze or orange leaves, while the white berries of *S. hupehensis* behind it contrast with the red foliage. In the shrubbery, viburnums, cotoneasters and berberis glisten with fruits and the leaves of *Parrotia persica* turn rich gold and crimson. Colchicums massed along the edge of the Wild Garden put in a dramatic appearance too. Chinese and Japanese witch hazels, *Hamamelis mollis* and *H. japonica* 'Superba', produce spidery, yellow, scented blooms from December onwards, when the winter sweet, *Chimonanthus praecox,* and *Lonicera* × *purpusii* contribute their heady fragrances.

In front of the Restaurant is a *Liriodendron tulipifera* planted by HM the Queen Mother in 1954, when she opened the Students' Hostel, Aberconway House, and the Restaurant. A small corner bed by the entrance demonstrates the effective use of foliage shrubs, with *Choisya ternata* 'Sundance', *Spiraea japonica* 'Gold Flame', the brownish red *Berberis thunbergii* 'Bagatelle', *Photinia* × *fraseri* 'Red Robin' and bright splashes of variegated euonymus and elaeagnus. Peonies, day lilies and irises spill over the borders under Aberconway House and climbing shrubs clamber up the walls. A new formal water feature is planned near here and island beds of herbaceous plants, grasses and modern shrub roses will be introduced.

The path leading back to the Laboratory passes a large bed devoted to ornamental grasses. The white, cream or silvery pink plumes of pampas grass, *Cortaderia selloana,* are unmistakable above the clumps of *Miscanthus sinensis*, some with arching sprays of flowers. The vivid green and yellow foliage of the dwarf bamboo, *Arundinaria viridistrata,* strikes an exotic note, while further contrasts of shape and colour, with purples, blues and reds, are provided by other grasses and fescues.

The Pinetum (26) and Howard's Field (27)

MANY visitors end their tour at the Restaurant and do not venture into the strip of land beyond, where the Pinetum and Howard's Field are situated. This area was closed to the public following the devastation of the 1987 and 1990 storms, when many notable trees were lost.

Out of all this upheaval has come the opportunity for major redevelopment. In the Pinetum, shrubs and trees chosen for autumn and spring colour, such as Japanese maples, witch hazels and flowering dogwoods, will be integrated with the existing conifers. Bold pockets of rhododendrons and evergreen azaleas are to be placed in the Pine Belt, leading through to Howard's Field.

Here, the establishment of the new heather garden is under way. An irrigation system has been set up and the soil prepared by incorporating copious quantities of manure and leafmould in what would otherwise be pure sand. The beds, divided by meandering paths, are being planted for visual impact, in groups of about 30 plants per cultivar. Eventually, there will be over 1,000 species and cultivars of *Erica, Calluna* and *Daboecia*, forming part of the National Collection. A refreshing change from the usual accompaniment of dwarf conifers will be the andromedas, cassiopes, gaultherias and dwarf sorbus. A collection of birches is also being planted. The transformation of Howard's Field promises to add yet another dimension to a great Garden.

Information Centre and Shop and Plant Centre

The Information Centre and Shop, next to the main entrance to the Garden, stocks an extensive range of gardening books, together with china, glass, stationery, gifts and other items, many of them exclusive to the Society.

The Plant Centre offers an extremely wide selection of hardy plants, including many unusual species and cultivars. Fruit trees, conservatory and house plants, bulbs and seeds are also available.

Both the Shop and the Plant Centre can be reached direct from the car park or from inside the Garden.

The Plant Centre (left) and the Information Centre and Shop (right)

Cover photograph by courtesy of Singapore Airlines Limited.

The majority of photographs used in the text are by Wilf Halliday, RHS Wisley.

Other photographs by:
John Garey, pp. 17, 34, 39, 59.
S. and O. Mathews, p. 3.
Kenneth Scowen, pp. 4, 18, 38, 55.
Michael Warren, Photos Horticultural, pp. 25, 53.
Don Wildridge, pp. 9, 10, 13, 19, 23, 24, 27, 50, 51.

Text by Fay Sharman, with the assistance of Jim Gardiner, Curator, and other staff at Wisley.

ISBN 0-906603-74-9

Designed and printed in Great Britain by Jarrold Printing, Norwich

Back cover: *Nyssa sylvatica* in Seven Acres in the autumn